Dear Parents/Caregivers:

Children learn to read in stages, and all children develop reading skills at different ages. **Fisher-Price® Ready Reader Storybooks**™ were created to encourage children's interest in reading and to increase their reading skills. The stories in this series were written to specific grade levels to serve the needs of children from preschool through third grade. Of course, every child is different, so we hope that you will allow your child to explore the stories at his or her own pace.

Book 1 and Book 2: Most Appropriate For Preschoolers

Book 3 and Book 4: Most Appropriate For Kindergartners

Book 5 and Book 6: Most Appropriate For First Graders

Book 7 and Book 8: Most Appropriate For Second Graders

Book 9 and Book 10: Most Appropriate For Third Graders

All of the stories in this series are fun, easy-to-follow tales that have engaging full-color artwork. Children can move from Books 1 and 2, which have the simplest vocabulary and concepts, to each progressive level to expand their reading skills. With the **Fisher-Price® Ready Reader Storybooks**™, reading will become an exciting adventure for your child. Soon your child will not only be ready to read, but will be eager to do so.

Educational Consultants: Mary McLean-Hely, M.A. in Education: Design and Evaluation of Educational Programs, Stanford University; Wendy Gelsanliter, M.S. in Early Childhood Education, Bank Street College of Education; Nancy A. Dearborn, B.S. in Education, University of Wisconsin-Whitewater

Ready Reader Storybook™

Jill's Glasses

Book 7

Written by Nancy Parent • Illustrated by Phyllis Harris

Modern Publishing
A Division of Unisystems, Inc.
New York, New York 10022

One day when Jill Bloom
went to school,

she couldn't read the
classroom rule.

Jill thought her eyes were getting worse so she went to see Miss Patch, the nurse.

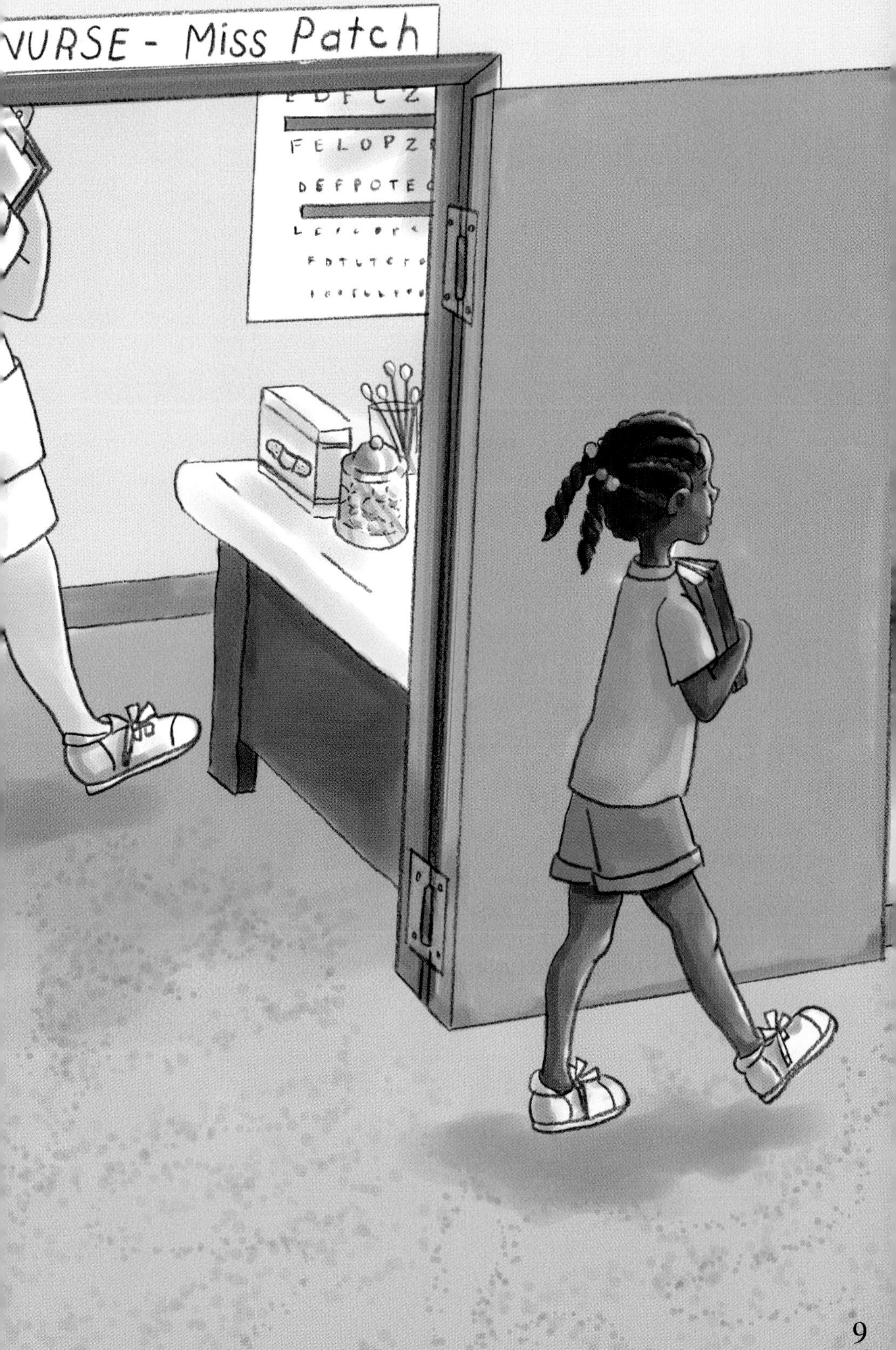
NURSE - Miss Patch

Jill read the chart and thought that "E" came right after the letter "C."

So Jill got glasses right away.

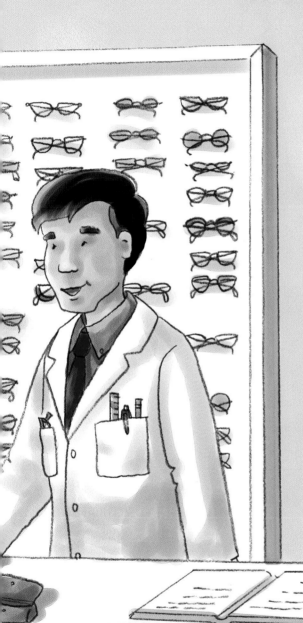
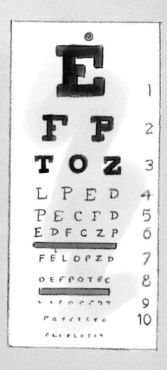

She put them on and cried,
"Hooray!"

Then Jill wondered how she would feel. Would wearing them be a big deal?

Jill was the only one in glasses
in either of the third grade classes.

She wore them every day
at school.

The other kids thought
she was cool.

Be considerate of others.

Jill felt so happy,
she cried, "Look!"

18

"Now I can read my
science book!"

Why, Jill could see the soccer ball,
and the goalie standing tall.

Jill wore glasses in the sun,
wearing them was really fun.

She kept her glasses on in bed.
"Please take them off," her
mother said.

But Jill was falling fast asleep
and she never even
heard a peep.

When Jill woke up, she couldn't see. Where, oh, where could her glasses be?

Jill looked high, and Jill looked low, but where they were, she didn't know.

She had to hurry or be late.
The school bus wasn't going
to wait.

Jill ran and got right on the bus.

The driver didn't make a fuss.

She quickly found an empty seat.

She almost tripped on
someone's feet.

She sat down next to her friend Ted, who found Jill's glasses on her head!